Chapter 1: Introduction to Machine Learning

Section 1.1: What is Machine Learning?

Machine learning is a subfield of artificial intelligence (AI) that focuses on the development of algorithms and models that enable computers to learn and make predictions or decisions without being explicitly programmed. It revolves around the idea of using data to automatically extract patterns, make inferences, and improve performance over time. Machine learning algorithms can be trained on large datasets to recognize complex patterns, solve intricate problems, and make accurate predictions.

Section 1.2: Historical Background

The concept of machine learning dates back to the mid-20th century when researchers began exploring ways to develop machines capable of learning from data. The pioneers in the field, including Arthur Samuel and Frank Rosenblatt, laid the foundation for early machine learning techniques. In 1956, the term "artificial intelligence" was coined, and machine learning emerged as a crucial aspect of AI research. Over the years, advancements in computing power, data availability, and algorithmic innovation have propelled machine learning into the forefront of modern technology.

Section 1.3: Machine Learning Paradigms

Machine learning can be broadly categorized into three paradigms: supervised learning, unsupervised learning, and reinforcement learning. Each paradigm tackles different learning scenarios and presents unique approaches to solving problems.

Section 1.3.1: Supervised Learning

Supervised learning is a machine learning paradigm where the algorithm learns from labeled data, meaning the training data has input features and corresponding target labels. The goal of supervised learning is to build a model that can accurately predict the correct label for unseen or future inputs. Examples of supervised learning algorithms include linear regression, decision trees, support vector machines (SVM), and neural networks. Supervised learning is commonly used in tasks such as image classification, speech recognition, and spam detection.

Section 1.3.2: Unsupervised Learning
Unsupervised learning, as the name suggests, involves learning from unlabeled data. In this paradigm, the algorithm aims to discover inherent patterns, structures, or relationships within the data without any predefined labels. Unsupervised learning algorithms can perform tasks like clustering, dimensionality reduction, and anomaly detection. Examples of unsupervised learning algorithms include k-means clustering, hierarchical clustering, principal component analysis (PCA), and generative adversarial networks (GANs).

Section 1.3.3: Reinforcement Learning
Reinforcement learning is a paradigm where an agent learns to interact with an environment and make decisions based on feedback in the form of rewards or punishments. The agent explores the environment, takes actions, and receives feedback to learn the optimal strategy that maximizes cumulative rewards. Reinforcement learning algorithms are commonly used in autonomous systems, game playing, robotics, and resource management problems. Notable reinforcement learning algorithms include Q-learning, deep Q-networks (DQN), and policy gradient methods.

In conclusion, machine learning is a powerful approach that allows computers to learn and make predictions without explicit programming. It encompasses various paradigms, including supervised learning, unsupervised learning, and reinforcement learning, each with its own set of techniques and applications. With the advent of big data and advancements in computational resources, machine learning has become instrumental in solving complex problems and driving innovation across industries.

Section 2.1: Data Representation and Preprocessing

Data representation and preprocessing involve transforming raw data into a format suitable for machine learning algorithms. Here are detailed explanations of the techniques and considerations covered in this section:

Data types: Different data types require specific preprocessing techniques. Numerical data represents continuous values and may need scaling or normalization to ensure that all features contribute equally to the model. Categorical data represents discrete categories and requires encoding to numerical values. Ordinal data has an inherent order, and text data may require special preprocessing techniques for feature extraction.

Data cleaning: Data cleaning involves handling missing values, outliers, and noise. Missing values can be addressed by imputation techniques such as mean imputation, median imputation, or using algorithms like K-Nearest Neighbors or regression to estimate missing values. Outliers, which are extreme values that deviate significantly from the other data points, can be detected and treated through techniques like Z-score, winsorization, or clustering-based approaches. Noise, which refers to random variations or errors in the data, can be reduced using smoothing techniques, filtering methods, or outlier removal techniques.

Feature scaling: Feature scaling ensures that all features have a similar range and do not dominate the learning process. Normalization scales data to a specific range, such as between 0 and 1 or -1 and 1. It is achieved by subtracting the minimum value and dividing by the range or by using techniques like min-max scaling. Standardization transforms data to have zero mean and unit variance, making it suitable for algorithms that rely on distance calculations or gradient-based optimization. It involves subtracting the mean and dividing by the standard deviation.

One-hot encoding and label encoding: Categorical variables need to be converted into numerical representations. One-hot encoding transforms each category into a binary column, where a value of 1 indicates the presence of that category and 0 indicates its absence. Label encoding assigns a unique numerical label to each category.

While one-hot encoding is suitable for nominal variables with no inherent order, label encoding is more appropriate for ordinal variables with an inherent order.

Handling imbalanced data: Imbalanced datasets, where one class is significantly more prevalent than others, can lead to biased models. Techniques for handling imbalanced data include oversampling the minority class by replicating samples, undersampling the majority class by removing samples, or using advanced methods like SMOTE (Synthetic Minority Over-sampling Technique) to generate synthetic samples for the minority class. Another approach is to use cost-sensitive learning algorithms that assign different misclassification costs to different classes.

Feature extraction: Feature extraction involves deriving new features from existing ones or transforming raw data into more meaningful representations. Dimensionality reduction techniques like Principal Component Analysis (PCA) or Singular Value Decomposition (SVD) can be used to extract the most important features that capture the most variance in the data. Other techniques include feature hashing for high-cardinality categorical variables, time-series feature extraction techniques, or text preprocessing techniques like tokenization, stemming, or stop-word removal.

Section 2.2: Feature Engineering

Feature engineering involves creating new features or transforming existing ones to enhance the performance of machine learning models. Here are detailed explanations of the techniques covered in this section:

Feature selection: Feature selection aims to select the most relevant features and reduce dimensionality. Univariate feature selection evaluates each feature independently and selects the top-k features based on statistical measures like ANOVA F-value, chi-square, or mutual information. Model-based feature selection uses a machine learning model to estimate the importance of each feature. Recursive Feature Elimination (RFE) recursively removes features based on their importance until a desired number of features is reached. L1-based regularization, such as Lasso, can also be used for feature selection by driving some feature coefficients to zero.

Feature creation: Feature creation involves generating new features from existing ones. This can be done through mathematical transformations, such as creating polynomial features by combining existing features using multiplication or exponentiation. Interaction terms can be created by multiplying two or more features to capture their combined effect. Domain knowledge and intuition play a crucial role in creating new features specific to the problem being solved. For example, in image processing, features can be created by calculating gradients, textures, or other visual characteristics.

Feature scaling: Feature scaling ensures that features are on a similar scale and prevents certain features from dominating the learning process. Scaling techniques like min-max scaling or standardization can be applied to features after feature engineering to bring them within a specific range or to have zero mean and unit variance.

Handling categorical variables: Categorical variables need to be converted into numerical representations suitable for machine learning models. One-hot encoding creates binary columns for each category, representing the presence or absence of a category in a sample. Ordinal encoding assigns numerical labels based on the order or ranking of categories, preserving the notion of the order or hierarchy. Feature hashing is another technique where categorical variables are hashed into a fixed-size vector, reducing the dimensionality and memory requirements.

Handling text data: Text data requires special preprocessing techniques for feature extraction. Tokenization breaks text into individual words or tokens, making it suitable for further processing. Stemming reduces words to their base or root forms to remove variations and improve generalization. Stop-word removal eliminates common, non-informative words that do not contribute much to the overall meaning. Techniques like TF-

IDF (Term Frequency-Inverse Document Frequency) can be used to represent text as numerical features by assigning weights to words based on their importance in a document or corpus. Word embeddings like Word2Vec or GloVe can capture semantic relationships between words by representing them as dense vectors in a continuous vector space.

Section 2.3: Model Evaluation and Selection

Model evaluation is crucial for assessing the performance of machine learning models. Here are detailed explanations of the evaluation metrics and techniques covered in this section:

Accuracy, precision, recall, F1-score, and ROC curves: Accuracy measures the overall correctness of predictions by dividing the number of correct predictions by the total number of predictions. Precision measures the proportion of true positives among the predicted positives, indicating the model's ability to avoid false positives. Recall measures the proportion of true positives identified by the model, indicating the model's ability to avoid false negatives. F1-score is the harmonic mean of precision and recall, providing a balanced measure of the model's overall performance. ROC (Receiver Operating Characteristic) curves visualize the trade-off between true positive rate (TPR) and false positive rate (FPR) at different classification thresholds.

Confusion matrix and classification report: A confusion matrix is a tabular representation of the model's predictions, showing the counts of true positives, true negatives, false positives, and false negatives. It provides insights into the model's performance for each class and can be used to calculate metrics like precision, recall, and F1-score. The classification report summarizes these metrics for each class, providing a comprehensive evaluation of the model's performance.

Regression metrics: Regression models require different evaluation metrics. Mean squared error (MSE) measures the average squared difference between predicted and actual values, providing a measure of the overall error. Root mean squared error (RMSE) is the square root of MSE, providing an interpretable metric in the original units of the target variable. Mean absolute error (MAE) measures the average absolute difference between predicted and actual values, providing a more robust measure against outliers. R-squared (coefficient of determination) measures the proportion of variance explained by the model, indicating its goodness of fit.

Model selection: Model selection involves comparing different models and selecting the best-performing one for a given task. Evaluation metrics like accuracy, F1-score, or R-squared can be used to compare models and choose the one that achieves the highest performance. Cross-validation or holdout validation can be used to estimate the model's performance on unseen data.

Hyperparameter tuning: Hyperparameters are parameters that are not learned from the data but are set manually before training the model. Hyperparameter tuning involves finding the optimal combination of hyperparameters to maximize model performance. Techniques like grid search, random search, or Bayesian optimization can be used to explore different combinations of hyperparameters and evaluate their impact on model performance.

Section 2.4: Bias-Variance Tradeoff

The bias-variance tradeoff is a fundamental concept in machine learning that balances model complexity and generalization. Here are detailed explanations of the concepts covered in this section:

Bias: Bias refers to the error introduced by overly simplistic assumptions made by the model. A high-bias model tends to underfit the data and may not capture the underlying patterns or relationships. It can result from using a model that is too simple or making strong assumptions about the data distribution. High-bias models have a tendency to oversimplify the relationships in the data, leading to poor performance on both the training and test sets.

Variance: Variance refers to the error caused by the model being too sensitive to the training data. A high-variance model tends to overfit the training data and may not generalize well to unseen data. High-variance models can capture noise or random fluctuations in the training data, leading to low training error but high test error. They have a tendency to be too complex and may fail to generalize to new, unseen examples.

Underfitting: Underfitting occurs when the model is too simple to capture the complexity of the underlying data. It typically results from using a model with low complexity or limited capacity. Underfit models have high bias and low variance, leading to both high training and test error. They fail to capture important patterns or relationships in the data and may require a more complex model or more informative features.

Overfitting: Overfitting occurs when the model excessively fits the noise or outliers in the training data, resulting in poor generalization to unseen data. It often happens when the model is too complex or has too many parameters relative to the available training data. Overfit models have low bias but high variance, leading to low training error but high test error. They can memorize the training data but fail to capture the underlying patterns, and they require regularization techniques or model simplification to generalize better.

Regularization techniques: Regularization is a technique used to control model complexity and mitigate overfitting. It involves adding penalty terms to the loss function to discourage large parameter values. L1 regularization (Lasso) adds the absolute value of the coefficients to the loss function, encouraging sparsity and feature selection. L2 regularization (Ridge) adds the square of the coefficients, promoting smaller and more evenly distributed coefficients. Regularization helps to find the right balance between bias and variance, reducing the risk of overfitting and improving model generalization.

Learning curves: Learning curves provide insights into the bias-variance tradeoff by plotting the training and validation error as a function of the training set size. By observing the learning curves, it is possible to determine whether the model is underfitting or overfitting. Underfitting is indicated by high training and validation error that plateaus as the training set size increases.

Overfitting is characterized by low training error but increasing validation error as the training set size increases. Learning curves can help identify the need for more data, model complexity adjustments, or regularization techniques.

Section 2.5: Overfitting and Underfitting

Overfitting and underfitting are common challenges in machine learning that affect the model's ability to generalize to unseen data. Here are detailed explanations of these phenomena and techniques to mitigate them:

Overfitting: Overfitting occurs when a model captures noise or outliers in the training data, leading to poor generalization to unseen data. It happens when the model is too complex or has too many parameters relative to the available training data. Overfit models have low bias but high variance, resulting in low training error but high test error. Techniques to mitigate overfitting include:

Regularization: Adding penalty terms to the loss function to limit the model's complexity and prevent overfitting. L1 and L2 regularization are commonly used regularization techniques.

Cross-validation: Evaluating the model's performance on different subsets of the data to estimate its generalization ability and detect overfitting. Techniques like k-fold cross-validation or holdout validation can be used.

Early stopping: Stopping the model training process when the validation error starts to increase, indicating that the model has started to overfit. This prevents the model from further learning noisy patterns in the training data.

Model simplification: Reducing the complexity of the model by reducing the number of parameters, decreasing the number of layers in a neural network, or using simpler algorithms that are less prone to overfitting.

Underfitting: Underfitting occurs when a model is too simple to capture the complexity of the underlying data. It typically results from using a model with low complexity or limited capacity.

Underfit models have high bias and low variance, resulting in both high training and test error. Techniques to mitigate underfitting include:

Increasing model complexity: Using a more complex model that can capture the underlying patterns in the data. This may involve increasing the number of parameters, adding more layers to a neural network, or using more expressive algorithms.
Feature engineering: Creating more informative features or transforming existing features to better represent the relationships in the data. This can help the model capture important patterns that were not evident in the original feature set.
Adding more training data: Increasing the size of the training set to provide the model with more diverse examples and a better chance to capture the underlying patterns. More data can help reduce the underfitting effect and improve model generalization.
Reducing regularization: If regularization is excessively limiting the model's capacity, reducing the strength of the regularization term or adjusting its hyperparameters can help alleviate underfitting.
Section 2.6: Cross-Validation
Cross-validation is a technique used to assess the performance and generalization ability of machine learning models. Here are detailed explanations of the concepts covered in this section:

k-fold cross-validation: In k-fold cross-validation, the data is divided into k subsets or folds. The model is trained on k-1 folds and evaluated on the remaining fold. This process is repeated k times, with each fold serving as the validation set exactly once. The performance metrics obtained from each fold can be averaged to obtain an estimate of the model's performance on unseen data.
Stratified k-fold cross-validation: Stratified k-fold cross-validation is used when dealing with imbalanced datasets, where one class is significantly more prevalent than others. It ensures that each fold contains a similar proportion of samples from each

class, providing a more representative evaluation of the model's performance.

Leave-one-out cross-validation: Leave-one-out cross-validation (LOOCV) is a special case of k-fold cross-validation where k is equal to the number of samples in the dataset. For each iteration, the model is trained on all samples except one, which is used for evaluation. LOOCV is suitable for small datasets but can be computationally expensive for larger datasets.

Cross-validation for time series data: Time series data has temporal dependencies that need to be taken into account when evaluating the model's performance. Techniques like forward chaining or rolling-window validation can be used, where the model is trained on past data and evaluated on future data.

Benefits and limitations of cross-validation: Cross-validation provides a more reliable estimate of the model's performance compared to a single train-test split. It helps assess the model's generalization ability and reduces the risk of overfitting. However, cross-validation can be computationally expensive, especially for large datasets or models that take a long time to train. It may also introduce some degree of data leakage if preprocessing steps, such as feature scaling or feature extraction, are applied to the entire dataset before cross-validation.

By understanding and applying the foundations of machine learning, including data preprocessing, feature engineering, model evaluation and selection, addressing the bias-variance tradeoff, and mitigating overfitting and underfitting, practitioners can build robust and accurate machine learning models for a wide range of applications. These concepts provide a solid foundation for further exploration and understanding of advanced machine learning techniques.

Section 3.1: Neural Networks: Building Blocks of Deep Learning
Neural networks are the building blocks of deep learning, enabling the extraction of intricate features from data. Let's dive into the fundamental concepts of neural networks in even greater detail:

Neurons: Neurons are the fundamental units of a neural network. They are inspired by the biological neurons in the human brain. In a neural network, a neuron takes inputs, applies weights to those inputs, and produces an output through an activation function. Each neuron operates on a simple principle, which involves computing a weighted sum of its inputs, applying an activation function to the sum, and passing the result to the next layer.

Layers: Neurons are organized into layers, forming the architecture of a neural network. The most common types of layers are the input layer, hidden layers, and output layer. The input layer receives the initial data and passes it to the hidden layers. The hidden layers process the information by performing mathematical operations on the inputs. Finally, the output layer produces the final results of the network's computation.

Connections: Neurons are interconnected through connections, which transmit information throughout the network. Each connection is associated with a weight that determines the strength of the connection. During the learning process, the weights are adjusted to optimize the network's performance. When information flows through the network during the forward propagation phase, the weighted inputs of each neuron are computed based on the inputs from the previous layer.

Architectures: Neural networks can have different architectures, each suited for specific tasks. Feedforward neural networks are the simplest and most commonly used type. They are called "feedforward" because the information flows in one direction, from the input layer to the output layer, without loops or feedback connections. Recurrent neural networks (RNNs) introduce feedback connections, allowing information to be passed from one step to the next. RNNs are suitable for tasks involving sequential data, such as natural language processing and time series analysis. Convolutional neural networks (CNNs) are designed specifically for processing grid-like data, such as images.

They leverage shared weights and convolutional operations to capture spatial patterns and hierarchies of features.

Section 3.2: Feedforward Neural Networks
Feedforward neural networks are the simplest form of neural networks. Let's explore their structure, components, and operations in greater detail:

Input layer, hidden layers, and output layer: A feedforward neural network typically consists of an input layer, one or more hidden layers, and an output layer. The input layer receives the initial data and passes it to the hidden layers. The hidden layers process the information by applying mathematical operations to the inputs. Finally, the output layer produces the final results of the network's computation.

Forward propagation: Forward propagation is the process of passing inputs through the network and computing outputs. It involves calculating the weighted sum of inputs at each neuron, applying an activation function to the sum, and passing the result to the next layer. This process is repeated layer by layer until the output layer is reached, and the final outputs of the network are obtained.

Activation functions: Activation functions introduce non-linearity into the network, enabling the network to learn complex mappings between inputs and outputs. Common activation functions include the sigmoid function, which squashes the input into a range between 0 and 1, and the hyperbolic tangent (tanh) function, which squashes the input between -1 and 1. These functions were traditionally used due to their smoothness and bounded output ranges. However, they suffer from the vanishing gradient problem, which can hinder the learning process. Rectified Linear Unit (ReLU) and its variants have gained popularity in recent years. ReLU applies the identity function to positive inputs and sets negative inputs to zero. ReLU is computationally efficient and allows for faster training of deep neural networks. Variants like Leaky ReLU and Parametric ReLU (PReLU) address the "dying ReLU" problem by introducing a small slope for negative inputs.

Network depth and width: The depth and width of a feedforward neural network impact its expressiveness and capacity. Depth refers to the number of hidden layers in the network, while width refers to the number of neurons in each layer. Increasing the depth and width of a network increases its capacity to represent complex relationships and capture intricate features in the data. However, a larger network also requires more computational resources and may be prone to overfitting if not properly regularized.

Section 3.3: Activation Functions
Activation functions play a crucial role in neural networks by introducing non-linearity and enabling complex representations. Let's delve even deeper into various activation functions commonly used in deep learning:

Sigmoid and hyperbolic tangent (tanh) functions: The sigmoid function is a smooth and bounded activation function that maps the input to a value between 0 and 1. It is often used in the output layer of a binary classification task, where it can represent the probability of belonging to a particular class. The tanh function is similar to the sigmoid function but maps the input to a value between -1 and 1. It can be used in both classification and regression tasks. Both sigmoid and tanh functions suffer from the vanishing gradient problem, which can slow down the learning process.

Rectified Linear Unit (ReLU) and its variants: Rectified Linear Unit (ReLU) is a widely used activation function that has gained popularity in deep learning. It applies the identity function to positive inputs, effectively outputting the input value itself. For negative inputs, ReLU sets the output to zero. ReLU is computationally efficient and allows for faster training of deep neural networks compared to sigmoid and tanh functions. However, ReLU can suffer from the "dying ReLU" problem, where a large fraction of neurons become inactive during training and produce zero outputs. To address this issue, variants like Leaky ReLU introduce a small slope for negative inputs, allowing some information to flow even for negative values. Parametric ReLU (PReLU) generalizes the leaky ReLU by learning the slope parameter during training.

Activation functions for specific use cases: Certain activation functions are specifically designed for particular tasks. The softmax function is commonly used in multi-class classification problems, where it normalizes the outputs of a neural network into a probability distribution over multiple classes. The output of softmax represents the predicted probabilities of each class, and the class with the highest probability is selected as the final prediction. The sigmoid function, which maps the input to a value between 0 and 1, is often used in binary classification tasks. It is suitable for problems where each sample belongs to one of two classes, and the output represents the probability of belonging to the positive class.

Section 3.4: Training Neural Networks: Backpropagation
Backpropagation is a key algorithm for training neural networks by adjusting the network's weights based on the error signal. Let's explore the backpropagation process in even greater detail:

Forward propagation: During forward propagation, inputs are passed through the neural network, and outputs are computed layer by layer. The weighted sum of inputs at each neuron is calculated, the activation function is applied, and the result is propagated to the next layer. The final outputs of the network are obtained from the output layer.

Loss function: A loss function measures the discrepancy between the predicted outputs and the true target values. It quantifies the error of the network's predictions and provides a feedback signal for adjusting the weights during backpropagation. The choice of the loss function depends on the specific task at hand. Mean squared error (MSE) is a common loss function used in regression tasks, where the goal is to minimize the average squared difference between predictions and targets. Categorical cross-entropy is often used in multi-class classification tasks, where it measures the dissimilarity between predicted class probabilities and true class labels. Binary cross-entropy is suitable for binary classification tasks.

Backward propagation: Backward propagation involves calculating the gradients of the loss function with respect to the network's weights. It starts from the output layer and moves backward, applying the chain rule to compute the derivative of the loss function with respect to each weight. The gradients indicate the direction and magnitude of the weight updates required to minimize the loss function. During backpropagation, the error signal is propagated through the network, and the gradients are calculated at each layer. The gradients provide information on how much each weight contributed to the overall error.

Gradient descent: Gradient descent is an optimization algorithm used to update the network's weights based on the computed gradients. It iteratively adjusts the weights in the direction opposite to the gradients to minimize the loss function. The magnitude of the weight update is determined by the learning rate, which determines the step size taken in each iteration. There are different variants of gradient descent, including batch gradient descent, mini-batch gradient descent, and stochastic gradient descent (SGD). In batch gradient descent, all training samples are used to compute the gradients and update the weights. Mini-batch gradient descent uses a subset of the training samples, and stochastic gradient descent updates the weights after processing each individual sample.

Chain rule: The chain rule is a fundamental mathematical concept used in backpropagation. It allows the calculation of gradients by recursively applying the derivatives of nested functions. In the context of neural networks, the chain rule is used to compute the gradients of the loss function with respect to the weights by propagating the error signal backward through the network. The chain rule ensures that the gradients can be efficiently computed layer by layer, starting from the output layer and moving backward.

Section 3.5: Loss Functions and Optimization Algorithms

Loss functions and optimization algorithms are vital for effectively training neural networks. Let's explore the common loss functions and optimization techniques used in deep learning in even greater detail:

Common loss functions: Loss functions measure the discrepancy between the predicted outputs and the true target values. Different tasks require different loss functions. Mean squared error (MSE) is a common loss function used in regression tasks, where the goal is to minimize the average squared difference between predictions and targets. MSE provides a measure of the average deviation of the predicted values from the true values. Categorical cross-entropy is often used in multi-class classification tasks. It quantifies the dissimilarity between the predicted class probabilities and the true class labels. Binary cross-entropy is suitable for binary classification tasks, where the goal is to minimize the dissimilarity between the predicted probability of belonging to the positive class and the true class label.

Regularization techniques: Regularization techniques are used to prevent overfitting, which occurs when a model performs well on the training data but fails to generalize to unseen data. L1 and L2 regularization are two commonly used techniques. L1 regularization, also known as Lasso regularization, adds a penalty term to the loss function that is proportional to the sum of the absolute values of the weights. This encourages sparsity in the weights, leading to feature selection and reducing the impact of less relevant features. L2 regularization, also known as Ridge regularization, adds a penalty term that is proportional to the sum of the squared values of the weights. This encourages smaller weights and leads to a more evenly distributed impact of features. Regularization techniques help control the complexity of the model and improve its generalization ability.

Optimization algorithms: Optimization algorithms determine how the network's weights are updated during training to minimize the loss function. Stochastic gradient descent (SGD) is a widely used optimization algorithm that updates the weights based on the gradients computed on small batches of training data. SGD is computationally efficient and can be parallelized, making it suitable for large-scale datasets. Adaptive learning rate algorithms, such as Adam (Adaptive Moment Estimation) and RMSprop (Root Mean Square Propagation), dynamically adjust the learning rate for each parameter based on the gradients. These algorithms maintain a moving average of the squared gradients and adjust the learning rate accordingly. Adaptive learning rate algorithms can speed up convergence and improve the stability of the training process.

Learning rate schedules and adaptive learning rates: The learning rate is a hyperparameter that determines the step size taken in weight updates during optimization. It plays a crucial role in the convergence and stability of the training process. Learning rate schedules adjust the learning rate over time to improve convergence or exploration. Common learning rate schedules include step decay, where the learning rate is reduced by a certain factor after a fixed number of epochs, and exponential decay, where the learning rate is exponentially decreased over time. Adaptive learning rate techniques dynamically adjust the learning rate based on the gradients or historical information. For example, AdaGrad adapts the learning rate for each parameter based on the sum of squared gradients encountered during training. Adaptive learning rate techniques can be useful in scenarios where different parameters have different scales or when dealing with sparse gradients.

By gaining a deeper understanding of the principles of neural networks, feedforward architectures, activation functions, backpropagation, and optimization, readers can develop a strong foundation in deep learning. These concepts provide the groundwork for building and training deep neural networks capable of handling complex tasks like image recognition, natural language processing, and more.

ection 4.1: Convolutional Neural Networks (CNN)
Convolutional Neural Networks (CNNs) are a class of deep learning architectures specifically designed for processing grid-like data, such as images or videos. Let's delve into even greater detail on the key components and operations of CNNs:

Convolutional layers: Convolutional layers are the primary building blocks of CNNs. Each convolutional layer consists of a set of learnable filters or kernels. These filters are small-sized matrices that slide over the input image in a systematic manner, computing the dot product between the filter weights and the corresponding local regions of the input. This process performs a convolution operation, which extracts relevant features by detecting patterns, edges, textures, or other visual elements. By applying multiple filters, the network can capture a variety of features at different spatial locations.

Pooling layers: Pooling layers are often inserted between consecutive convolutional layers to reduce the spatial dimensions of the feature maps while preserving the essential information. The most commonly used pooling technique is max pooling, which downsamples the feature maps by selecting the maximum value within a predefined neighborhood or pooling window. Max pooling helps to achieve translation invariance by focusing on the most salient features while discarding less relevant details. Other pooling methods, such as average pooling, compute the average value instead.

Activation functions and non-linearities in CNNs: Activation functions introduce non-linearity to the CNN, enabling the network to learn complex representations. In CNNs, activation functions are applied element-wise to the outputs of convolutional or pooling layers. Rectified Linear Unit (ReLU) is a widely used activation function in CNNs due to its simplicity and effectiveness. ReLU sets all negative values to zero and leaves positive values unchanged, introducing sparsity and non-linearity. Other activation functions, such as sigmoid and tanh, can also be used, particularly in the output layer for specific tasks.

Common CNN architectures: Several notable CNN architectures have significantly contributed to the advancement of deep learning. LeNet-5, proposed by Yann LeCun, was one of the earliest successful CNNs and achieved impressive results in handwritten digit recognition. AlexNet, introduced by Alex Krizhevsky et al., gained attention after winning the ImageNet Large-Scale Visual Recognition Challenge (ILSVRC) in 2012. Its deep architecture and the use of ReLU activation functions propelled the field forward. VGGNet, developed by the Visual Geometry Group, emphasized deeper networks by using small convolutional filters (3x3) with multiple stacked layers, achieving high accuracy. ResNet (Residual Network) utilized skip connections or shortcuts to address the vanishing gradient problem in very deep networks, enabling the training of networks with hundreds of layers.

Transfer learning with pre-trained CNN models: Transfer learning leverages pre-trained CNN models that have been trained on large-scale datasets, such as ImageNet, to tackle new tasks with limited data. Instead of training a CNN from scratch, transfer learning allows practitioners to utilize the learned features and transfer them to a new task or domain. By freezing the weights of the pre-trained layers and retraining only the last few layers or adding new layers on top, transfer learning enables the efficient training of models on smaller datasets, accelerates convergence, and improves generalization performance.

Applications of CNNs: CNNs have achieved remarkable success in various computer vision tasks. Image classification, which involves assigning labels to images, has been revolutionized by CNNs. Notable examples include the ImageNet challenge, where CNN-based models have surpassed human-level performance. Object detection, which focuses on localizing and classifying multiple objects within an image, has also greatly benefited from CNN architectures like Faster R-CNN, YOLO (You Only Look Once), and SSD (Single Shot MultiBox Detector). Image segmentation, which aims to assign semantic labels to each pixel in an image, has seen significant advancements with CNN-based architectures such as U-Net and Mask R-CNN. CNNs have also made significant contributions to facial recognition, image synthesis, medical image analysis, autonomous driving, and many other computer vision applications.

Section 4.2: Recurrent Neural Networks (RNN)
Recurrent Neural Networks (RNNs) are designed to handle sequential and temporal data, making them suitable for tasks like natural language processing and time series analysis. Let's explore even greater detail on RNNs:

Recurrent connections and hidden states: RNNs possess recurrent connections that allow information to flow in cycles, enabling the network to retain information about previous inputs. At each time step, the current input and the previous hidden state are combined to produce the current hidden state. The hidden state acts as the memory or context of the network, allowing it to capture dependencies and contextual information across time. RNNs maintain a hidden state that serves as an internal representation of the past inputs and influences the predictions or outputs at each time step.

Vanishing gradient problem in traditional RNNs: Traditional RNNs can suffer from the vanishing gradient problem, where the gradients diminish exponentially as they propagate backward through time during training. This problem arises due to the repeated multiplication of gradient values during backpropagation, which can lead to unstable training and difficulties in capturing long-term dependencies. In cases where gradients vanish, the network struggles to learn and propagate information across distant time steps.

Long Short-Term Memory (LSTM): LSTM is an RNN variant designed to address the vanishing gradient problem and capture long-term dependencies more effectively. LSTM introduces memory cells, which enable the network to selectively retain or forget information over time. LSTM cells contain three crucial components: an input gate, a forget gate, and an output gate. These gates regulate the flow of information and control how much information from the current input, previous hidden state, and previous cell state should be stored, forgotten, or outputted. By allowing for controlled information flow, LSTM can capture dependencies over longer sequences and mitigate the issues associated with vanishing gradients.

Gated Recurrent Units (GRU): GRU is another RNN variant similar to LSTM but with a simplified architecture. GRU combines the forget and input gates of LSTM into a single update gate and merges the cell state and hidden state. The simplified structure of GRU reduces the number of gating parameters and computational complexity compared to LSTM while still capturing long-term dependencies effectively. GRU has demonstrated competitive performance in various sequence-related tasks and is often used as a more computationally efficient alternative to LSTM.

Bidirectional RNNs: Bidirectional RNNs process sequences in both forward and backward directions, allowing the network to capture information from past and future contexts. This is achieved by duplicating the hidden states and processing the sequence in both directions independently. By considering both past and future contexts, bidirectional RNNs can access comprehensive information and improve the understanding of the input sequence. Bidirectional RNNs have been successful in tasks such as part-of-speech tagging, named entity recognition, sentiment analysis, and machine translation.

Applications of RNNs: RNNs have found applications in various domains. In machine translation, RNN-based architectures like the Sequence-to-Sequence (Seq2Seq) model with attention mechanisms have achieved state-of-the-art performance. RNNs have been instrumental in sentiment analysis, where the goal is to determine the sentiment or emotion expressed in textual data. Speech recognition systems leverage RNNs to convert spoken language into written text. Handwriting recognition, time series analysis, and generative models for text and music are other areas where RNNs have demonstrated significant impact and utility.

Section 4.3: Transformers
Transformers have revolutionized the field of natural language processing (NLP) and achieved state-of-the-art results in tasks like language translation and language generation. Let's explore even greater detail on the key components and innovations of transformer architectures:

Self-attention mechanism: The self-attention mechanism is a fundamental building block of transformers. It allows the model to capture relationships between different positions in a sequence. Unlike traditional recurrent connections that process information sequentially, self-attention allows the model to attend to all positions in the input sequence simultaneously. By calculating attention weights between all pairs of positions, the model can capture dependencies and focus on relevant context within the sequence.

Multi-head attention: Multi-head attention is an extension of the self-attention mechanism that enables the model to learn multiple representations and capture different aspects of the input sequence. In multi-head attention, the self-attention mechanism is applied in parallel multiple times, each with its own set of learned parameters or attention weights. The outputs of the different attention heads are then concatenated or linearly transformed to form the final representation. Multi-head attention enhances the model's ability to capture diverse patterns and relationships within the input sequence.

Positional encoding: Transformers do not have inherent notions of order or position in the input sequence. To incorporate positional information, positional encoding is used. Positional encoding provides the model with a way to differentiate between different positions in the sequence. Typically, sine and cosine functions with different frequencies are used to encode positional information and are added to the input embeddings. The positional encodings allow the model to understand the relative and absolute positions of the tokens in the sequence.

Transformer encoder and decoder architectures: Transformers consist of an encoder-decoder architecture. The encoder processes the input sequence, while the decoder generates the output sequence autoregressively. The encoder consists of multiple stacked layers, each composed of a multi-head self-attention mechanism and a feed-forward neural network. The self-attention mechanism captures dependencies within the input sequence, and the feed-forward network provides additional nonlinear transformations. The decoder shares a similar structure but also incorporates an additional encoder-decoder attention mechanism to attend to the encoder's output representation.

Transformer-based models: Several transformer-based models have achieved remarkable success in NLP tasks. BERT (Bidirectional Encoder Representations from Transformers) introduced the concept of masked language modeling and next sentence prediction. BERT pretrains a transformer model on large amounts of unlabeled text data and fine-tunes it on downstream tasks. GPT (Generative Pre-trained Transformer) and

GPT-2 employ transformer decoders to generate coherent and contextually relevant text based on a given prompt. T5 (Text-to-Text Transfer Transformer) is a versatile transformer model that can be trained on a wide range of NLP tasks by framing them as text-to-text problems.

Applications of transformers: Transformers have excelled in various NLP tasks. Machine translation, where the goal is to translate text from one language to another, has witnessed significant improvements with transformer-based architectures. Question answering systems, sentiment analysis, text summarization, and document classification are other areas where transformers have achieved state-of-the-art performance. Transformers have also been applied to image captioning, speech recognition, dialogue systems, and various creative applications like poetry generation and text completion.

Section 4.4: Autoencoders and Variational Autoencoders
Autoencoders are unsupervised learning models used for dimensionality reduction, data compression, and generative modeling. Variational Autoencoders (VAEs) extend traditional autoencoders by introducing probabilistic modeling to the latent space. Let's explore even greater detail on these architectures:

Encoder and decoder components in autoencoders: Autoencoders consist of an encoder and a decoder. The encoder takes the input data and maps it to a lower-dimensional representation called the latent space or bottleneck layer. The decoder then reconstructs the original input from the latent space representation. The goal of an autoencoder is to learn a compressed representation of the data that captures the most important features. By reducing the dimensionality, autoencoders can learn efficient representations and remove noise or irrelevant details from the input.

Bottleneck layer: The bottleneck layer or latent space is a low-dimensional representation of the input data in the autoencoder. It serves as a compressed encoding that captures the most salient features of the data. By compressing the data into a lower-dimensional space, autoencoders facilitate dimensionality reduction, data compression, and feature extraction.

Reconstruction loss: The reconstruction loss measures the fidelity of the reconstructed inputs compared to the original inputs. It quantifies the difference between the original data and the data reconstructed by the decoder. Common reconstruction loss functions include mean squared error (MSE) for continuous data and binary cross-entropy for binary data. The autoencoder aims to minimize the reconstruction loss during training, which encourages the network to capture the essential information necessary for faithful reconstruction.

Latent space and sampling in VAEs: Variational Autoencoders (VAEs) introduce probabilistic modeling to the latent space of autoencoders. Rather than directly encoding data into a fixed lower-dimensional representation, VAEs map the data to the parameters of a probability distribution, typically a multivariate Gaussian distribution. The latent space is defined by the mean and variance (or other parameters) of the distribution. During training, VAEs learn to encode the input data into these parameters, enabling the generation of new data points by sampling from the learned latent space distribution.

Loss function and the role of the Kullback-Leibler (KL) divergence in VAEs: VAEs employ a loss function that combines the reconstruction loss and the Kullback-Leibler (KL) divergence. The reconstruction loss measures the fidelity of the reconstructed inputs, ensuring that the decoder can faithfully reconstruct the original inputs. The KL divergence measures the difference between the learned distribution in the latent space and a predefined prior distribution, often a standard Gaussian. The KL divergence regularizes the latent space and encourages it to follow a known distribution, aiding in generating new samples from the learned distribution.

Applications of autoencoders and VAEs: Autoencoders and VAEs have found applications in various domains. In image generation, VAEs can generate new images by sampling from the learned latent space. Autoencoders are used for dimensionality reduction, where the compressed representation can be visualized or used for downstream tasks. Anomaly detection involves using autoencoders to reconstruct normal instances and identify outliers or anomalies based on large reconstruction errors. VAEs have been used in data synthesis, generating realistic samples of complex data distributions, and as generative models for creative applications like music and art.

By diving into these intricate details of deep learning architectures, including CNNs, RNNs, transformers, autoencoders, and VAEs, practitioners can develop a comprehensive understanding of their inner workings and their respective applications. This in-depth knowledge empowers researchers and practitioners to explore the full potential of these architectures, adapt them to specific tasks, and drive innovation in the field of deep learning.

Section 5.1: Image Classification
Image classification is a fundamental task in computer vision, and deep learning has revolutionized its accuracy and performance. Let's delve even deeper into the intricacies of image classification with deep learning:

Convolutional Neural Networks (CNNs) for image classification: CNNs have become the go-to architecture for image classification due to their ability to effectively capture spatial hierarchies and local patterns in images. CNNs consist of multiple layers, including convolutional layers, pooling layers, and fully connected layers. The convolutional layers apply filters to the input image, extracting features that represent different levels of abstraction. Pooling layers reduce the spatial dimensions, aggregating the extracted features. Finally, fully connected layers classify the image based on the learned features.

Dataset preparation and augmentation techniques: Preparing the dataset is crucial for training accurate image classification models. This involves collecting a diverse and representative dataset, splitting it into training and validation sets, and often including a separate test set for final evaluation. Data augmentation techniques help increase the dataset's size and variability, enhancing the model's ability to generalize to unseen data. Augmentation techniques include random cropping, flipping, rotation, scaling, and brightness adjustment.

Training strategies and optimization algorithms: Training deep learning models for image classification typically involves iterative optimization processes. Stochastic Gradient Descent (SGD) is a popular optimization algorithm used to update the model's weights based on the gradients of the loss function. Learning rate scheduling techniques, such as step decay, exponential decay, or adaptive learning rates, can help improve convergence and avoid getting stuck in suboptimal solutions. Other optimization algorithms, such as Adam, RMSprop, and Adagrad, offer adaptive learning rate schemes and momentum to accelerate training.

Evaluation metrics for image classification: Various evaluation metrics assess the performance of image classification models. Accuracy, the most commonly used metric, measures the percentage of correctly classified images in the test set. Precision, recall, and F1-score provide more detailed insights by considering the true positive, false positive, and false negative rates. Receiver Operating Characteristic (ROC) curves visualize the trade-off between true positive rate and false positive rate at different classification thresholds. Area Under the Curve (AUC) summarizes the overall performance of the classifier.

State-of-the-art architectures and models for image classification: Deep learning has witnessed the development of state-of-the-art architectures and models that push the boundaries of image classification performance. ResNet (Residual Network) introduced residual connections, which help alleviate the vanishing gradient problem and enable training of very deep networks. InceptionNet utilizes a combination of different-sized convolutions and parallel branches to capture multi-scale features. EfficientNet employs compound scaling to achieve high accuracy with efficient model sizes.

Section 5.2: Object Detection

Object detection involves identifying and localizing objects within an image. Deep learning has revolutionized object detection, enabling accurate and real-time detection. Let's explore object detection in even greater detail:

Region-based approaches: Region-based methods divide the object detection task into two stages: region proposal generation and region classification. R-CNN (Region-based Convolutional Neural Network) introduced this paradigm by generating region proposals using selective search or region proposal networks (RPNs). These proposals are then classified using CNNs. Fast R-CNN improved upon R-CNN by sharing the computation for the region proposals and introducing ROI (Region of Interest) pooling. Faster R-CNN further optimized the process by integrating RPNs directly into the network architecture.

Single-shot approaches: Single-shot methods aim to detect objects in a single pass through the network, making them faster but still accurate. YOLO (You Only Look Once) divides the input image into a grid and predicts bounding boxes and class probabilities directly from each grid cell. YOLOv2 and YOLOv3 introduced anchor boxes of different scales and aspect ratios to handle objects of various sizes. SSD (Single Shot MultiBox Detector) employs a series of convolutional layers with different scales and aspect ratios to detect objects at multiple scales.

Anchor-based and anchor-free methods: Object detection

approaches can be categorized as anchor-based or anchor-free. Anchor-based methods assign predefined anchor boxes to regions of the image and predict offsets and class probabilities for these anchors. This approach allows handling objects of various scales and aspect ratios. RetinaNet and EfficientDet are examples of anchor-based methods. Anchor-free methods, on the other hand, directly predict bounding boxes without relying on predefined anchors. CenterNet and CornerNet fall into this category.

Evaluation metrics for object detection: Object detection performance is evaluated using metrics such as Intersection over Union (IoU), which measures the overlap between predicted and ground-truth bounding boxes. Average Precision (AP) is commonly used to summarize detection performance across different IoU thresholds. Mean Average Precision (mAP) combines AP values at various IoU thresholds to provide an overall performance metric. Precision-Recall curves visualize the trade-off between precision and recall at different detection thresholds.

Recent advancements in object detection: Recent advancements in object detection have focused on improving accuracy, speed, and efficiency. EfficientDet utilizes efficient backbone networks and compound scaling to achieve high accuracy with fewer parameters and computations. Cascade R-CNN introduces a multi-stage cascade architecture, refining object proposals and classification results in multiple stages. DETR (DEtection TRansformer) replaces the traditional anchor-based detection pipeline with a transformer-based architecture, achieving state-of-the-art performance.

Section 5.3: Semantic Segmentation
Semantic segmentation aims to assign semantic labels to each pixel in an image, enabling detailed understanding of the image's structure. Let's delve even deeper into semantic segmentation with deep learning:

Fully Convolutional Networks (FCNs) for semantic segmentation:

Fully Convolutional Networks (FCNs) are designed specifically for semantic segmentation tasks, allowing the network to produce pixel-wise predictions. FCNs replace the fully connected layers of traditional CNN architectures with convolutional layers to preserve spatial information. Skip connections or skip architecture are often incorporated to combine feature maps from different levels of abstraction, enabling precise localization of objects while preserving fine details.

Encoder-Decoder architectures: U-Net and SegNet are popular encoder-decoder architectures for semantic segmentation. U-Net consists of an encoder path, which gradually reduces the spatial dimensions to capture context, and a decoder path, which upsamples the feature maps to produce dense pixel-wise predictions. SegNet, on the other hand, uses an architecture that mirrors the encoder-decoder structure, but it incorporates pooling indices from the encoder path to guide the upsampling process.

Dilated convolutions and atrous spatial pyramid pooling: Dilated convolutions, also known as atrous convolutions, have been instrumental in semantic segmentation. They allow the network to have a larger receptive field without increasing the number of parameters, effectively capturing larger context information. Atrous spatial pyramid pooling (ASPP) extends this idea by using dilated convolutions at multiple rates, capturing multi-scale context information.

Evaluation metrics for semantic segmentation: Evaluation metrics for semantic segmentation include Intersection over Union (IoU), also known as Jaccard Index, which measures the pixel-wise overlap between predicted and ground-truth regions. Mean Intersection over Union (mIoU) computes the average IoU across all classes. Pixel Accuracy measures the percentage of correctly classified pixels. Frequency Weighted Intersection over Union (FWIoU) accounts for class imbalance by weighing the IoU values based on the class frequencies.

State-of-the-art models for semantic segmentation: DeepLab is a state-of-the-art semantic segmentation model that incorporates dilated convolutions and atrous spatial pyramid pooling to capture rich contextual information. DeepLabv3+ integrates a powerful feature extraction backbone with atrous spatial pyramid pooling and a decoder module for precise boundary delineation. PSPNet (Pyramid Scene Parsing Network) uses pyramid pooling modules to capture multi-scale contextual information and has achieved impressive performance on various benchmark datasets.

Section 5.4: Instance Segmentation

Instance segmentation goes beyond semantic segmentation by not only assigning semantic labels to each pixel but also differentiating individual objects and providing precise spatial information. Let's dive even deeper into instance segmentation with deep learning:

Mask R-CNN: Mask R-CNN combines object detection and semantic segmentation to achieve instance segmentation. It extends the Faster R-CNN architecture by adding a mask prediction branch to generate segmentation masks for each detected object. The additional mask branch operates in parallel with the bounding box and class prediction branches, allowing precise delineation of object boundaries and accurate identification of individual instances within an image.

Panoptic segmentation: Panoptic segmentation aims to unify semantic and instance segmentation by assigning a unique label to each pixel in the image, providing both semantic understanding and spatial information. Panoptic FCN and Panoptic FPN are popular frameworks for panoptic segmentation. Panoptic FCN extends the FCN architecture by incorporating an additional branch to predict semantic labels. Panoptic FPN introduces a fusion module that combines instance and semantic features, enabling end-to-end panoptic segmentation.

Evaluation metrics for instance segmentation: Evaluation

metrics for instance segmentation include metrics for both detection and segmentation. For detection, metrics such as Average Precision (AP) and mean Average Precision (mAP) are used to assess the accuracy of object localization and classification. For segmentation, metrics such as Mask Intersection over Union (Mask IoU) measure the pixel-wise overlap between predicted masks and ground-truth masks. Panoptic Quality (PQ) is a metric specifically designed for panoptic segmentation, combining object detection, segmentation, and overlap-aware matching.

Recent advancements and models for instance segmentation: Recent advancements in instance segmentation have focused on improving accuracy, efficiency, and integration with panoptic segmentation. BlendMask is an anchor-based instance segmentation model that integrates the advantages of both one-stage and two-stage methods, achieving competitive performance with low computational cost. HTC (Hybrid Task Cascade) introduces a multi-stage cascade architecture that refines instance segmentation masks in multiple stages, leading to improved localization and accuracy. These advancements have pushed the boundaries of instance segmentation and opened up possibilities for more precise and detailed scene understanding.

Section 5.5: Generative Adversarial Networks (GANs) in Computer Vision

Generative Adversarial Networks (GANs) have revolutionized computer vision by enabling the generation of realistic images. Let's explore GANs in even greater detail:

GAN architecture and components: GANs consist of two main components: a generator network and a discriminator network. The generator network takes random noise as input and learns to generate synthetic images. The discriminator network, on the other hand, aims to distinguish between real and synthetic images. The two networks play a minimax game, with the generator learning to generate more realistic images that fool the discriminator, while the discriminator learns to correctly classify real and generated images.

Training GANs: GANs are trained using an adversarial loss function. During training, the generator and discriminator networks are updated iteratively. The generator aims to minimize the adversarial loss by generating images that are indistinguishable from real images, while the discriminator aims to maximize the adversarial loss by correctly classifying real and generated images. This process creates a competitive dynamic where the generator continually improves its ability to generate realistic images, while the discriminator becomes more skilled at distinguishing between real and generated images.

Conditional GANs and image-to-image translation: Conditional GANs extend the basic GAN framework by conditioning the generator and discriminator on additional input variables, such as class labels or input images. This enables controlled generation or translation of images based on specific conditions. Conditional GANs have been widely used for image-to-image translation tasks, such as style transfer, image colorization, image super-resolution, and domain adaptation. By conditioning the generator on specific input conditions, conditional GANs provide fine-grained control over the generated images' attributes and characteristics.

StyleGAN and StyleGAN2: StyleGAN and StyleGAN2 are advanced GAN architectures that have significantly advanced the quality and diversity of generated images. StyleGAN introduces a style-based generator architecture that disentangles the latent space into style and content representations. The style vectors control various attributes and details of the generated images, allowing for precise manipulation of features like facial expressions, colors, and styles. StyleGAN2 further improves upon the original architecture by introducing a more stable training procedure and refining the generation process.

Evaluation metrics for GANs: Evaluating the quality and diversity of generated images is challenging since there is no ground truth for comparison. However, several evaluation metrics have been proposed to assess GAN performance. Inception Score measures the quality and diversity of generated images based on the predictions of an Inception model. Fréchet Inception Distance (FID) compares the distributions of real and generated images based on feature statistics extracted from a pre-trained Inception model. These metrics provide quantitative measures to evaluate and compare different GAN models.

GANs have significantly advanced the field of computer vision by enabling the generation of highly realistic and diverse images. The combination of generator and discriminator networks in an adversarial framework has revolutionized image generation and opened up possibilities for applications such as image synthesis, image editing, data augmentation, and content creation.

Section 5.6: Transfer Learning in Computer Vision
Transfer learning leverages pre-trained models and knowledge from one task or domain to another, enabling effective training with limited data and improving performance. Let's delve even deeper into transfer learning in computer vision:

Pre-trained models and their architectures: Pre-trained models are deep learning models that have been trained on large-scale datasets, such as ImageNet. These models capture general visual features and can serve as a starting point for various computer vision tasks. Common pre-trained models include VGG (Visual Geometry Group), ResNet (Residual Network), Inception, and MobileNet, each with its own architecture, depth, and performance characteristics.

Fine-tuning and transfer learning strategies: Fine-tuning involves taking a pre-trained model and adapting it to a specific task or dataset. The process typically involves freezing some layers, such as the initial layers responsible for low-level feature extraction, and only updating the weights of the later layers. This allows the model to retain the general visual knowledge learned from the pre-training while adapting to the specific task. Transfer learning strategies may also involve using pre-trained models as feature extractors, where the output of the pre-trained model is used as input to another model for the task at hand.

Domain adaptation and transfer learning across different datasets: Domain adaptation refers to the process of transferring knowledge from a source domain to a target domain with different characteristics. In computer vision, this often involves training a model on a source dataset and adapting it to perform well on a target dataset with different distributions or conditions. Techniques such as domain adversarial training, where the model learns to align feature distributions between the source and target domains, can be used to improve transfer learning performance across different datasets.

Practical considerations and best practices for transfer learning in computer vision: When applying transfer learning, it is important to consider factors such as the similarity between the source and target tasks, the size of the target dataset, and the availability of computational resources. The choice of pre-trained model architecture, the layers to freeze or fine-tune, and the learning rate schedule should be carefully determined based on the specific task and dataset. It is also essential to conduct proper evaluation and validation to ensure that the transfer learning approach improves performance and generalization.

Transfer learning in computer vision has been instrumental in overcoming the limitations of limited labeled data and resource constraints. By leveraging pre-trained models and transferring knowledge across tasks and domains, transfer learning enables the efficient training of accurate and robust computer vision models. It has become a standard practice in various computer vision applications, including object detection, image classification, and semantic segmentation.

Section 6.4: Sequence-to-Sequence Models and Language Translation

Sequence-to-Sequence (Seq2Seq) models have been widely used for language translation and other NLP tasks. Let's delve even deeper into Seq2Seq models and language translation:

Encoder-Decoder architectures for machine translation: Seq2Seq models consist of two main components: an encoder and a decoder. The encoder processes the input sequence, such as a source sentence in the source language, and encodes it into a fixed-length representation called the context vector or latent representation. The decoder then generates the output sequence, such as a target sentence in the target language, based on the encoded context vector. This architecture enables the model to capture the input sequence's semantic and syntactic information and generate an appropriate output sequence.

Attention mechanisms in Seq2Seq models: Attention mechanisms have significantly improved the performance of Seq2Seq models, especially in long sequences or cases where the input and output sequences have different lengths. Attention mechanisms allow the model to focus on relevant parts of the input sequence while generating the output sequence. By assigning different attention weights to different parts of the input sequence, the model can attend to the most relevant information at each decoding step. Common attention mechanisms include additive attention, multiplicative attention, and self-attention.

Beam search for decoding translations: Beam search is a decoding technique used in Seq2Seq models to generate translations or decode the output sequence. Instead of greedily selecting the most likely word at each decoding step, beam search explores multiple candidate paths and keeps track of the top-k most likely sequences. This technique helps to mitigate the issue of getting stuck in suboptimal solutions and encourages the model to explore alternative translations.

Handling rare or out-of-vocabulary words: Seq2Seq models may encounter rare or out-of-vocabulary (OOV) words during the translation process. To handle such cases, techniques like replacing OOV words with a special token or using an external dictionary or language model for OOV words can be employed. Additionally, subword tokenization techniques, such as Byte Pair Encoding (BPE) or SentencePiece, can be used to handle rare or unknown words by splitting them into smaller units that are more likely to be known to the model.

Training and evaluation of Seq2Seq models for language translation: Seq2Seq models are typically trained using pairs of source and target sequences, where the goal is to minimize the discrepancy between the generated output sequence and the target sequence. Training involves optimizing the model parameters using techniques like teacher forcing, where the true target sequence is provided as input during training. Evaluation of Seq2Seq models for language translation is often done using metrics such as BLEU (Bilingual Evaluation Understudy) or METEOR (Metric for Evaluation of Translation with Explicit ORdering).

Section 6.5: Attention Mechanisms in NLP
Attention mechanisms have significantly improved the performance of NLP models by allowing them to focus on important parts of the input. Let's explore attention mechanisms in NLP in even greater detail:

Self-attention and scaled dot-product attention: Self-attention, also known as intra-attention, allows a model to attend to different positions within the same input sequence. It computes attention weights by comparing each input element to all other elements in the sequence. Scaled dot-product attention is a commonly used mechanism for self-attention, where attention weights are calculated based on the dot product between the query and key vectors, scaled by a factor to prevent large values.

Multi-head attention for capturing different relationships: Multi-head attention extends the basic attention mechanism by employing multiple sets of attention weights, called attention heads. Each attention head attends to different parts of the input sequence, enabling the model to capture different relationships and dependencies. The attention outputs from multiple heads are then concatenated or linearly transformed to obtain the final output.

Transformer architecture and its use of attention mechanisms: The Transformer architecture, introduced in the "Attention Is All You Need" paper, revolutionized NLP models. It combines self-attention layers with feed-forward layers to capture both local and global dependencies. The Transformer eliminates the need for recurrent or convolutional structures, making it more parallelizable and efficient for training. Transformers have been successful in various NLP tasks, including machine translation, question answering, and text generation.

Applications of attention mechanisms in NLP tasks: Attention mechanisms have been widely applied in various NLP tasks. For example, in sentiment analysis, attention mechanisms can identify the most influential words or phrases in determining the sentiment of a sentence. In question answering, attention can highlight relevant parts of the input passage when generating an answer. Attention has also been used in tasks like text summarization, natural language inference, and document classification to improve model performance and interpretability.

Section 6.6: Transformer-based Models: BERT and GPT
Transformer-based models have made significant advancements in NLP tasks, achieving state-of-the-art results. Let's focus on two prominent models:

BERT (Bidirectional Encoder Representations from Transformers): BERT introduced the concept of masked language modeling and transformed the field of NLP. It is a pre-trained model that learns contextual representations of words by randomly masking some of the words in the input and predicting them based on the surrounding context. BERT's bidirectional nature allows it to capture context from both left and right contexts, leading to better contextual understanding and representation learning. BERT has been fine-tuned for a wide range of NLP tasks, such as text classification, named entity recognition, and question answering.

GPT (Generative Pre-trained Transformer): GPT is a generative language model based on the Transformer architecture. It is trained on a large corpus of text data and can generate coherent and contextually relevant text given a prompt. GPT models use an autoregressive approach, where the model generates one word at a time based on the previously generated words. GPT has been used for tasks like text completion, dialogue generation, and story generation.

Transfer learning with pre-trained transformer models: Pre-trained transformer models like BERT and GPT have revolutionized transfer learning in NLP. By leveraging large-scale pre-training on diverse text corpora, these models capture a wealth of linguistic knowledge and can be fine-tuned on specific downstream tasks with limited labeled data. Fine-tuning involves updating the model's parameters on the task-specific dataset while retaining the pre-trained knowledge. Transfer learning with pre-trained transformer models has significantly improved performance across various NLP tasks and reduced the need for extensive task-specific training data.

Evaluation metrics for NLP tasks and benchmarks: NLP tasks are evaluated using various metrics depending on the specific task. For example, text classification tasks may use metrics such as accuracy, precision, recall, or F1-score. Machine translation tasks often use metrics like BLEU (Bilingual Evaluation Understudy) or METEOR (Metric for Evaluation of Translation with Explicit ORdering) to evaluate the quality of the generated translations. Evaluation benchmarks like GLUE (General Language Understanding Evaluation) or SQuAD (Stanford Question Answering Dataset) provide standardized datasets and evaluation protocols for a wide range of NLP tasks.

By delving into the principles and techniques discussed in this chapter, practitioners can gain a deep understanding of natural language processing and deep learning. This knowledge enables them to develop and fine-tune advanced NLP models, apply attention mechanisms effectively, leverage transformer-based architectures like BERT and GPT, and achieve state-of-the-art results in various NLP tasks.

User
more details and more in depth
ChatGPT
Section 6.1: Text Preprocessing
Text preprocessing is a crucial step in NLP that involves transforming raw text into a format suitable for deep learning models. Let's explore the techniques and considerations in even greater detail:

Tokenization: Tokenization is the process of breaking down a text into individual words or tokens. It involves splitting the text based on spaces or punctuation marks. In some cases, tokenization may involve more complex rules to handle special cases like contractions or hyphenated words. Tokenization is the fundamental step for representing text as numerical input for deep learning models.

Stop-word removal: Stop words are common words that do not carry much meaning, such as "and," "the," or "is." These words can be removed from the text during preprocessing to reduce noise and focus on more informative words. However, the removal of stop words should be done carefully as they might carry importance in certain contexts or tasks.

Stemming and lemmatization: Stemming and lemmatization are techniques used to reduce words to their base or root forms. Stemming involves removing prefixes or suffixes from words to obtain the core root form. Lemmatization, on the other hand, takes into consideration the word's part of speech and applies morphological analysis to obtain the base form. For example, the words "running," "runs," and "ran" would all be reduced to the lemma "run."

Handling special characters, punctuation, and numerical values: Text preprocessing should also consider how to handle special characters, punctuation marks, and numerical values. Special characters and punctuation marks can be removed or replaced, depending on the specific requirements of the task. Numerical values can be standardized or replaced with a special token to maintain the numerical information without introducing unnecessary complexity.

Handling rare or misspelled words: In some cases, the text may contain rare or misspelled words that are not present in the pre-trained word embeddings or vocabulary. These words can be replaced with a special token to indicate their rarity or handled separately during model training and evaluation. Techniques like character-level embeddings or subword tokenization can also help handle out-of-vocabulary words.

Text normalization techniques: Text normalization involves transforming text to a standardized format. This may include converting text to lowercase, removing accents or diacritical marks, or normalizing certain conventions like expanding contractions ("can't" to "cannot"). Normalization ensures consistency in the text representation and reduces the complexity of the vocabulary.

Section 6.2: Word Embeddings: Word2Vec and GloVe
Word embeddings play a crucial role in NLP by capturing the semantic and syntactic relationships between words. Let's delve

even deeper into word embeddings:

Word2Vec: Word2Vec is a popular word embedding model that learns distributed representations of words based on their co-occurrence in a large corpus of text. There are two main architectures in Word2Vec: Continuous Bag of Words (CBOW) and Skip-gram. CBOW predicts a target word based on its surrounding context words, while Skip-gram predicts context words given a target word. Word2Vec models capture semantic relationships by representing words with dense vectors in a high-dimensional space, where similar words are closer together.

Training word embeddings on large corpora: Word2Vec models are typically trained on large corpora of text, such as Wikipedia articles or news data, to capture a wide range of linguistic patterns and relationships. The training process involves adjusting the word vectors to maximize the model's ability to predict context words given a target word or vice versa. The training objective is often based on maximizing the likelihood of the observed word-context pairs.

GloVe (Global Vectors for Word Representation): GloVe is another popular word embedding model that uses word co-occurrence statistics to learn word representations. GloVe leverages the idea that word vectors should encode not only the local context of a word but also the global distributional patterns of its co-occurrences. By considering the word co-occurrence matrix, GloVe models capture both local and global word relationships, resulting in more nuanced embeddings.

Pre-trained word embeddings and their applications: Pre-trained word embeddings, such as Word2Vec and GloVe, provide a valuable resource for NLP tasks, especially when the available training data is limited. These pre-trained embeddings capture general language patterns and can be used as initialization for downstream tasks or fine-tuned on specific domain or task-specific data. Pre-trained embeddings are particularly useful when the target task lacks sufficient labeled data to train word embeddings from scratch.

Evaluation of word embeddings and similarity measures: Word embeddings can be evaluated using various intrinsic and extrinsic evaluation measures. Intrinsic evaluation measures assess the quality of word embeddings based on their ability to capture semantic or syntactic relationships, such as word similarity or analogy tasks. Extrinsic evaluation measures assess the impact of word embeddings on downstream tasks like text classification or sentiment analysis. Similarity measures, such as cosine similarity or Euclidean distance, can be used to quantify the similarity between word vectors and evaluate their quality.

Section 6.3: Recurrent Neural Networks for Text Classification
Recurrent Neural Networks (RNNs) are powerful models for sequential data processing, including text classification. Let's explore the application of RNNs in text classification in greater detail:

Word-level and sentence-level classification: Text classification can be performed at different granularities, such as word-level or sentence-level. Word-level classification assigns a label to each individual word, while sentence-level classification assigns a label to the entire sentence or document. RNNs can be applied to both word-level and sentence-level classification tasks by considering the sequential nature of the input.

Long Short-Term Memory (LSTM) and Gated Recurrent Units (GRU) for text classification: LSTM and GRU are popular variants of RNNs that address the vanishing gradient problem and allow for capturing long-term dependencies in sequential data. LSTM introduces memory cells and gates to selectively store and retrieve information, while GRU simplifies the architecture by using fewer gates. Both LSTM and GRU have shown promising results in text classification tasks by capturing the contextual information and understanding the sequence of words in a sentence.

Handling variable-length inputs using padding and masking: Text sequences in a dataset may have different lengths, but RNNs require fixed-length inputs. To handle variable-length inputs, padding can be used to make all sequences the same length by adding special padding tokens. Additionally, masking can be applied to ignore the padded tokens during computation, ensuring that the model focuses only on the relevant parts of the input sequences.

Training strategies and optimization algorithms for RNNs: Training RNNs involves optimizing the model's parameters to minimize a loss function. Gradient descent algorithms, such as Stochastic Gradient Descent (SGD), Adam, or RMSprop, can be used to update the model's parameters based on the gradients computed through backpropagation. Techniques like dropout, batch normalization, or gradient clipping can be employed to improve the model's generalization, stability, and convergence during training.

Transfer learning and fine-tuning for text classification tasks: Transfer learning can be applied to text classification tasks by leveraging pre-trained RNN models on large-scale datasets or pre-trained word embeddings. Fine-tuning involves adapting the pre-trained models or embeddings to the target task by updating the parameters on the task-specific dataset. Transfer learning and fine-tuning can significantly reduce the need for extensive training data and improve the performance of text classification models, especially in scenarios where labeled data is limited.

By delving into the principles and techniques discussed in this chapter, practitioners can gain a deeper understanding of NLP and deep learning. This knowledge equips them with the skills to preprocess text effectively, generate meaningful word embeddings, leverage RNNs for text classification, and overcome challenges like variable-length inputs and training strategies. With these advanced techniques, practitioners can develop sophisticated NLP models capable of handling various tasks, such as sentiment analysis, text generation, machine translation, and more.

Section 7.4: Policy Gradient Methods

Policy gradient methods are a class of reinforcement learning algorithms that directly optimize the agent's policy to maximize the expected cumulative rewards. Let's delve into policy gradient methods in more detail:

Policy parameterization: In policy gradient methods, the agent's policy is typically parameterized by a function approximator, such as a neural network. The parameters of the policy network are updated to improve the policy's performance. The policy can be stochastic, with probabilities assigned to different actions, or deterministic, with a single action selected based on the policy's output.

Policy gradients and likelihood ratio gradient estimator: The key idea behind policy gradients is to estimate the gradient of the expected cumulative rewards with respect to the policy parameters. The likelihood ratio gradient estimator is commonly used to estimate this gradient. It involves computing the gradients of the log-probabilities of the actions taken multiplied by the cumulative rewards. This estimator provides a principled way to update the policy parameters in the direction of higher expected rewards.

REINFORCE algorithm: The REINFORCE algorithm is a well-known policy gradient method that uses Monte Carlo sampling to estimate the expected cumulative rewards. It involves collecting trajectories by interacting with the environment, computing the gradients of the log-probabilities and cumulative rewards for each trajectory, and updating the policy parameters using the gradient ascent rule. REINFORCE is an unbiased estimator of the policy gradient but suffers from high variance due to the Monte Carlo sampling.

Baseline and advantage functions: To reduce the variance of policy gradient estimates, a baseline function is often subtracted from the cumulative rewards. The baseline provides a measure of the expected rewards under the current policy. Additionally, advantage functions can be used to estimate the advantages of taking different actions compared to the baseline. Subtracting the advantage function from the cumulative rewards further reduces the variance and helps focus the policy updates on actions that yield higher-than-expected rewards.

Section 7.5: Proximal Policy Optimization (PPO)

Proximal Policy Optimization (PPO) is an advanced policy optimization algorithm that addresses some of the challenges of traditional policy gradient methods. Here are more details about PPO:

Clipped surrogate objective: PPO introduces a clipped surrogate objective function to limit the policy update to a certain range. The objective function combines a surrogate loss term, which approximates the policy gradient, and a constraint term. By clipping the surrogate loss, PPO prevents large policy updates that can destabilize the learning process. The constraint term ensures that the policy update stays within a trust region, defined by a hyperparameter.

Trust region and adaptive learning rates: PPO operates within a trust region, which determines the allowable range of policy updates. The trust region can be seen as a safety constraint that prevents drastic policy changes. To handle the trust region, PPO uses an adaptive learning rate mechanism. The learning rate is adjusted based on the ratio between the new policy and the old policy, ensuring that the policy update remains within the trust region.

PPO variants: Different variants of PPO have been proposed to improve its performance and address specific challenges. PPO-

Clip is the original variant, which uses the clipped surrogate objective. PPO-Penalty introduces an additional penalty term in the objective function to enforce a stricter constraint on policy updates. PPO-Lagrangian incorporates a Lagrange multiplier to balance the objective and constraint. These variants offer different trade-offs between stability and policy update magnitude.

Importance of hyperparameters and tuning in PPO: PPO's performance is highly sensitive to the choice of hyperparameters, including the clipping range, learning rate, value function coefficient, and entropy coefficient. Proper tuning of these hyperparameters is crucial for achieving good performance and stable learning. Researchers often employ techniques such as grid search, random search, or automated hyperparameter optimization to find optimal hyperparameter settings.

Empirical performance and applications of PPO: PPO has demonstrated strong empirical performance in various reinforcement learning tasks, including continuous control, robotic manipulation, and game playing. It has been successfully applied to complex environments and has achieved state-of-the-art results on benchmark tasks, such as the OpenAI Gym and Atari games. PPO's stability, sample efficiency, and ease of implementation have contributed to its popularity in the field of reinforcement learning.

By understanding the intricacies of policy gradient methods and the advancements introduced by PPO, practitioners can apply these techniques effectively in reinforcement learning scenarios. Policy gradient methods provide a flexible and powerful approach for training agents in complex environments, and PPO, with its trust region, adaptive learning rates, and clipped surrogate objective, offers a robust and stable optimization algorithm. These advancements pave the way for developing intelligent agents capable of learning complex behaviors and making optimal decisions in diverse domains.

Section 8.1: Explainable AI (XAI)

Explainable AI (XAI) is a field of research dedicated to developing machine learning models and techniques that provide transparency and interpretability. Here are more detailed explanations of XAI concepts:

Importance of interpretability: Interpretability is crucial in domains where decisions made by AI systems have significant impact on individuals or society, such as healthcare, finance, and autonomous vehicles. Interpretable models allow users to understand the reasoning behind the system's decisions, detect biases or errors, and ensure fairness, accountability, and compliance with regulations.

Local and global interpretability: Local interpretability focuses on explaining individual predictions or decisions made by the model. It provides insight into how a particular input influenced the model's output. Global interpretability, on the other hand, aims to understand the overall behavior of the model and its decision-making process across multiple inputs.

Rule-based explanations and decision trees: Rule-based explanations provide interpretable rules or logical conditions that explain the model's predictions. Decision trees are a widely used interpretable model that partitions the feature space based on simple if-then rules. The paths in a decision tree can be easily interpreted, providing transparency in decision-making.

Model-agnostic methods: Model-agnostic XAI methods aim to explain the predictions of any machine learning model, regardless of its architecture or complexity. LIME (Local Interpretable Model-Agnostic Explanations) generates local explanations by approximating the behavior of a complex model with an interpretable model in a local neighborhood around the prediction. SHAP (SHapley Additive exPlanations) applies concepts from cooperative game theory to attribute feature importance to individual predictions.

Interpreting deep neural networks: Deep neural networks are powerful models with multiple layers and millions of parameters, making them less interpretable. XAI research focuses on developing methods to interpret and explain the predictions of deep neural networks. Techniques such as saliency maps, gradient-based methods, and occlusion analysis help visualize which parts of the input contribute most to the model's decision.

Challenges and trade-offs: XAI faces challenges such as the interpretability-performance trade-off. Highly interpretable models like decision trees may sacrifice some predictive accuracy compared to more complex models like deep neural networks. Balancing interpretability and performance is an ongoing research challenge. Additionally, different stakeholders may have different requirements for interpretability, and XAI methods need to be flexible enough to address diverse needs while maintaining transparency.

Section 8.2: Generative Models: Variational Autoencoders and Generative Adversarial Networks (GANs)

Generative models aim to learn the underlying data distribution and generate new samples that resemble the training data. Here are deeper explanations of generative models:

Variational Autoencoders (VAEs): VAEs are probabilistic generative models that combine the power of autoencoders and variational inference. VAEs consist of an encoder network that maps input data to a latent space and a decoder network that reconstructs the input from the latent space. The encoder learns the parameters of the latent distribution, allowing the model to generate new samples by sampling from the learned latent space. VAEs provide a principled way to perform inference and generate samples from complex data distributions.

Generative Adversarial Networks (GANs): GANs are a class of

generative models that employ a game-theoretic framework to train a generator network and a discriminator network simultaneously. The generator network generates synthetic samples, while the discriminator network tries to distinguish between real and synthetic samples. The two networks play a minimax game, with the generator aiming to generate realistic samples that deceive the discriminator, and the discriminator aiming to accurately classify real and synthetic samples. Through adversarial training, GANs learn to generate high-quality samples that closely resemble the training data.

Conditional and unconditional generation: Generative models can be trained for unconditional generation, where samples are generated without any conditioning information. They can also be trained for conditional generation, where samples are generated based on specific conditions or attributes. Conditional generation allows fine-grained control over the generated samples, enabling the generation of samples with desired attributes or styles.

Applications of generative models: Generative models have numerous applications. In image synthesis, they can generate novel images with desired characteristics or generate missing parts of images. They are also used for data augmentation, generating additional training samples to increase the diversity of the dataset and improve model generalization. Generative models are employed in anomaly detection by modeling the normal data distribution and identifying deviations from it. They are also used in style transfer, image-to-image translation, and content generation.

Challenges in training and evaluation: Training generative models can be challenging. Mode collapse, where the generator produces limited variations of samples, is a common issue. Evaluating generative models is also challenging, as there is no ground truth for generated samples. Evaluation metrics such as Inception Score and Fréchet Inception Distance (FID) are used to assess the quality and diversity of generated samples.

Understanding the deeper nuances of XAI and generative models allows practitioners to develop models with interpretability and generate samples that resemble real data. These advanced techniques enable trust, transparency, and control in AI systems while providing the ability to generate new samples with desired attributes and styles.

Section 9.1: Bias and Fairness in Machine Learning

Bias and fairness are critical considerations in machine learning systems as they can have significant social and ethical implications. Here are more detailed explanations of bias and fairness in machine learning:

Sources of bias: Bias can arise from various sources, including biased data collection methods, historical biases in the data, and biased algorithmic decisions. Biases can manifest in different forms, such as racial or gender bias, and can lead to unfair outcomes for certain groups.

Fairness definitions and metrics: Fairness in machine learning can be defined in different ways, depending on the context and desired outcomes. Common fairness metrics include demographic parity, equal opportunity, and equalized odds, which measure the fairness of predictions across different groups.

Challenges in achieving fairness: Achieving fairness in machine learning models is challenging due to trade-offs between fairness and other desirable properties, such as accuracy and utility. Striving for fairness may result in reduced predictive performance or exclusion of certain groups from benefits. Balancing these trade-offs requires careful consideration and ethical judgment.

Mitigation techniques: Various techniques can help mitigate bias and improve fairness in machine learning models. Algorithmic auditing involves assessing the fairness of models and algorithms using statistical methods and metrics. Fairness-aware learning algorithms aim to explicitly optimize fairness objectives during the model training process.

Importance of diverse and representative datasets: Diverse and representative datasets are crucial for addressing bias in machine learning. Ensuring diversity in training data helps avoid underrepresentation and provides fair treatment to all groups. It is essential to consider the potential biases present in the data and take steps to mitigate them.

Fairness considerations in sensitive domains: Sensitive domains like criminal justice and healthcare require special attention to fairness. Biased predictions or decisions can have severe consequences, such as perpetuating discrimination or denying equitable access to healthcare services. Ensuring fairness in these domains is critical to avoiding harm and upholding ethical standards.

Section 9.2: Privacy and Data Protection

Privacy and data protection are significant ethical concerns in machine learning, particularly in the context of handling personal and sensitive data. Here are deeper explanations of privacy and data protection considerations:

Data privacy and informed consent: Respecting individuals' privacy rights involves obtaining informed consent for data collection, storage, and usage. Individuals should be aware of the types of data collected, the purposes for which they will be used, and their rights regarding their personal information.

Data anonymization and de-identification techniques: Anonymization and de-identification techniques aim to protect individuals' privacy by removing or altering personally identifiable information from datasets. Methods like k-anonymity, differential privacy, and data masking help reduce the risk of re-identification while preserving data utility.

Privacy risks in data sharing and aggregation: Sharing

and aggregating data can pose privacy risks, especially when combining datasets from multiple sources. Aggregation techniques, such as federated learning and secure multi-party computation, can mitigate privacy risks by allowing collaborative analysis without sharing raw data.

GDPR and other privacy regulations: The General Data Protection Regulation (GDPR) is a comprehensive data protection regulation that sets guidelines for the collection, storage, and processing of personal data in the European Union. Other regions and countries have similar privacy regulations that aim to protect individuals' rights and ensure responsible data handling.

Differential privacy: Differential privacy is a privacy-enhancing framework that provides mathematical guarantees of privacy protection. It introduces controlled noise or perturbation to query responses to protect individuals' privacy while enabling useful analysis of the data.

Secure computation techniques: Secure computation techniques, such as secure multiparty computation (MPC) and homomorphic encryption, enable computations on encrypted data without exposing sensitive information. These techniques ensure data privacy and protect sensitive information during computation.

Section 9.3: Transparency and Explainability

Transparency and explainability are crucial for building trust, accountability, and understanding in machine learning systems. Here are more detailed explanations of transparency and explainability considerations:

Interpretable machine learning models and algorithms: Interpretable models, such as decision trees and linear models, are inherently transparent as their inner workings can be easily understood. Using interpretable models can help explain the reasoning behind the model's predictions or decisions.

Model-agnostic interpretability techniques: Model-agnostic

interpretability techniques aim to explain the predictions of any machine learning model, regardless of its complexity. Techniques like LIME (Local Interpretable Model-Agnostic Explanations) and SHAP (SHapley Additive exPlanations) generate explanations by approximating the behavior of the model around specific instances.

Explanations for black-box models: Black-box models, such as deep neural networks, lack inherent interpretability. Researchers have developed methods to explain the predictions of black-box models, including rule-based explanations, attribution methods, and saliency maps, which highlight the input features that influenced the model's decision.

Importance of human-readable explanations: Human-readable explanations are vital in decision-making contexts, as they enable stakeholders to understand and evaluate the reasoning behind the model's predictions or decisions. Providing explanations in understandable terms fosters trust, accountability, and user acceptance of AI systems.

Trade-offs between transparency and model complexity: Highly complex models, such as deep neural networks, often sacrifice interpretability for improved predictive performance. There is a trade-off between model complexity and transparency, and finding the right balance depends on the context and the stakeholders' requirements.

Challenges in explainability in deep learning models: Deep neural networks have millions of parameters and intricate architectures, making their inner workings challenging to interpret. Research efforts are focused on developing techniques to explain and understand the decisions made by deep learning models, such as visualizing feature importance and identifying influential neurons or layers.

Section 9.4: Accountability and Responsibility

Accountability and responsibility are fundamental considerations in the development and deployment of machine learning systems. Here are deeper explanations of accountability and responsibility in machine learning:

Ethical implications of automated decision-making: Automated decision-making systems have ethical implications as they can impact individuals' lives and welfare. Understanding the potential consequences and biases of AI systems is essential to ensure responsible decision-making and prevent harm.

Legal and regulatory frameworks for AI accountability: Legal and regulatory frameworks aim to hold individuals and organizations accountable for the development and deployment of AI systems. These frameworks establish guidelines and requirements for transparency, fairness, privacy, and accountability in AI technologies.

Role of human oversight and intervention: Human oversight and intervention play a critical role in ensuring ethical AI. Humans should have the ability to review and challenge AI decisions, especially in critical domains such as healthcare and criminal justice, where the stakes are high. Humans can provide context, domain knowledge, and ethical judgment that machines may lack.

Algorithmic biases and impact on decision-making: Algorithms can inadvertently perpetuate biases present in the data used for training. Bias in decision-making can lead to unfair or discriminatory outcomes. Identifying and mitigating algorithmic biases is essential to ensure fairness and prevent unintended harm.

Responsible AI development and deployment practices: Organizations and practitioners should follow responsible AI development and deployment practices. This includes conducting thorough testing and validation, considering potential biases and ethical implications, involving diverse perspectives in the development process, and continuously monitoring and addressing issues that arise.

Addressing unintended consequences and risks: AI systems can have unintended consequences and risks. Understanding the potential societal impact, conducting risk assessments, and taking measures to address and mitigate risks are necessary to ensure the responsible and ethical deployment of AI technologies.

Section 9.5: Ensuring Ethical AI Systems

Ensuring ethical AI systems requires a comprehensive approach throughout the machine learning pipeline. Here are strategies and considerations for ensuring ethical AI systems:

Ethical AI principles and guidelines: Developing and following ethical AI principles and guidelines helps establish a foundation for responsible AI development and deployment. These principles provide guidance on fairness, transparency, accountability, and privacy.

Ethical review boards and frameworks: Establishing ethical review boards or committees can help organizations ensure that their AI systems align with ethical standards. These boards can assess the ethical implications, risks, and potential harms associated with AI projects and provide guidance for responsible practices.

Ethical considerations throughout the machine learning pipeline: Ethical considerations should be integrated into all stages of the machine learning pipeline. From data collection and preprocessing to model development, validation, and deployment, ethical considerations should guide decision-making and ensure responsible practices.

Ethical decision-making frameworks: Ethical decision-making frameworks, such as value-sensitive design or consequentialist approaches, provide structured methods for evaluating the ethical implications of AI systems. These frameworks help identify potential ethical dilemmas, assess risks, and make informed decisions.

Ongoing monitoring and evaluation: Continuously monitoring and evaluating AI systems for ethical concerns is crucial. Regular audits, feedback loops, and mechanisms for reporting and addressing ethical issues should be established to ensure that AI systems evolve responsibly and address emerging challenges.

Collaborative efforts and interdisciplinary research: Promoting collaboration among AI researchers, policymakers, ethicists, and stakeholders from diverse domains helps foster interdisciplinary research and collective efforts to address ethical considerations. Collaborative initiatives can drive the development of guidelines, best practices, and regulatory frameworks for responsible AI.

By considering and addressing issues related to bias, fairness, privacy, transparency, accountability, and responsibility, practitioners can ensure the development and deployment of ethical AI systems. Ethical considerations are essential not only from a legal and regulatory standpoint but also for building trust, protecting individuals' rights, and ensuring the fair and responsible use of AI technologies.

Section 10.1: Cutting-Edge Research and Developments

Machine learning is a field of ongoing research and development, with new breakthroughs and areas of exploration emerging constantly. Here are more detailed explanations of cutting-edge research and developments in machine learning:

Deep reinforcement learning: Deep reinforcement learning combines deep neural networks with reinforcement learning algorithms to enable agents to learn from high-dimensional sensory inputs and make complex decisions. This area has seen significant advancements, with breakthroughs like AlphaGo and OpenAI Five achieving superhuman performance in complex games.

Meta-learning and few-shot learning: Meta-learning focuses on developing models that can quickly adapt to new tasks with limited data. Few-shot learning aims to train models that can generalize from only a few examples. These areas have the potential to enable more efficient and adaptive machine learning systems that can learn new tasks with minimal data.

Explainable and interpretable AI: There is a growing need for AI systems that can provide explanations for their decisions and actions. Research in explainable and interpretable AI focuses on developing models and techniques that can provide transparent and understandable explanations for the reasoning behind AI decisions. This is particularly important in domains where interpretability is crucial, such as healthcare and legal applications.

Multi-modal learning: Multi-modal learning involves integrating information from different data modalities, such as text, images, and audio, to achieve a richer understanding of the data. This area holds promise for applications that require a comprehensive understanding of complex data, such as multimodal sentiment analysis, image captioning, and video analysis.

Quantum machine learning: Quantum computing has the potential to revolutionize machine learning by leveraging quantum principles to enhance computational capabilities. Quantum machine learning explores the use of quantum algorithms and quantum simulators to solve complex optimization and inference problems more efficiently.

Integration with other emerging technologies: Machine learning is increasingly integrated with other emerging technologies, such as robotics, augmented reality, and quantum computing. These integrations enable the development of intelligent systems with enhanced capabilities, such as robotic perception and control, immersive augmented reality experiences, and quantum-enhanced machine learning algorithms.

Section 10.2: Advances in Hardware and Accelerators

Advancements in hardware significantly impact the capabilities and efficiency of machine learning systems. Here are deeper explanations of the impact of hardware developments on machine learning:

GPUs (Graphics Processing Units): GPUs have played a crucial role in accelerating deep learning computations due to their parallel processing capabilities. GPUs enable training and inference on large-scale deep neural networks by efficiently performing matrix operations required for neural network computations.

ASICs and FPGAs: Application-specific integrated circuits (ASICs) and field-programmable gate arrays (FPGAs) offer specialized hardware architectures designed for specific machine learning tasks. These hardware accelerators provide efficient and customized solutions for tasks like computer vision, natural language processing, and recommendation systems.

TPUs and dedicated accelerators: Tensor Processing Units (TPUs) are Google's custom-designed hardware accelerators specifically optimized for deep learning workloads. TPUs deliver high computational performance and energy efficiency, enabling faster training and inference for deep neural networks. Other dedicated accelerators, such as neuromorphic chips and analog computing devices, are also being explored for specialized machine learning tasks.

Quantum computing: Quantum computing has the potential to revolutionize machine learning by leveraging quantum principles, such as superposition and entanglement, to perform computations more efficiently than classical computers. Quantum machine learning algorithms are being developed to harness the power of quantum computing for solving complex optimization and inference problems.

Edge computing: Edge computing involves bringing machine learning capabilities closer to the data source, reducing the need for extensive data transfers to central servers or the cloud. This approach enables real-time and low-latency inference on resource-constrained devices, making it suitable for applications that require rapid decision-making or privacy-sensitive data processing, such as edge AI in autonomous vehicles and smart homes.

Section 10.3: Challenges and Opportunities in AI

As machine learning progresses, several challenges and opportunities arise. Here are deeper explanations of key challenges and opportunities in AI:

Data quality and bias: Ensuring high-quality data that is representative and unbiased remains a challenge. Biases present in training data can result in biased or discriminatory AI systems. Addressing data quality issues and mitigating bias are essential for building fair and reliable machine learning models.

Robustness and generalization: Machine learning models need to perform well in diverse and complex real-world scenarios. Achieving robustness and generalization requires addressing challenges such as adversarial attacks, domain shift, and data scarcity to ensure models can handle novel situations and generalize well beyond their training data.

Data privacy and security: Protecting individuals' privacy and ensuring the security of sensitive data are crucial considerations in AI. Safeguarding data from unauthorized access or misuse and implementing privacy-preserving techniques, such as secure computation and differential privacy, are vital for maintaining trust and complying with privacy regulations.

Continual learning and lifelong adaptation: Enabling machine learning models to continuously learn and adapt to new information and evolving environments is an ongoing challenge.

Continual learning techniques that can overcome catastrophic forgetting and support efficient updating of models with new data are areas of active research.

Ethical considerations and responsible AI development and deployment: The ethical implications of AI systems require careful consideration throughout the entire machine learning lifecycle. Responsible AI development practices, adherence to ethical guidelines, and the establishment of regulatory frameworks are necessary to ensure AI is developed and deployed in a manner that respects human values, fairness, and societal well-being.

Collaboration and interdisciplinary approaches: AI challenges often require interdisciplinary collaboration between experts in machine learning, ethics, law, and various domains. Collaborative efforts can help address complex challenges, foster innovation, and ensure that AI technologies are developed in a manner that aligns with societal needs and values.

Section 10.4: Ethical and Societal Implications

The rapid advancement of machine learning brings ethical and societal implications that require careful consideration. Here are more detailed explanations of the ethical and societal considerations in AI:

Impact on employment and workforce: The increasing automation of tasks through AI and machine learning raises concerns about job displacement and the need for upskilling or reskilling the workforce. Understanding the implications for employment and creating strategies to address potential job displacement are important for ensuring a smooth transition and equitable distribution of opportunities.

Algorithmic biases and fairness in decision-making: Machine learning models can inherit biases present in the data they are trained on, leading to unfair or discriminatory outcomes.

Addressing algorithmic biases and ensuring fairness in decision-making processes are crucial to avoid reinforcing existing societal biases or discriminating against certain groups.

Transparency and accountability of AI systems: Ensuring transparency and accountability of AI systems is essential for building trust and understanding. Making AI systems transparent and providing mechanisms for accountability and recourse can help address concerns related to bias, errors, and unethical behavior in AI decision-making.

Ethical use of AI in critical domains: AI applications in critical domains such as healthcare and criminal justice require careful consideration of ethical and societal implications. Striking the right balance between efficiency, fairness, privacy, and human oversight is necessary to ensure the ethical use of AI and prevent potential harm to individuals or society.

Social and economic implications: AI technologies have broader social and economic implications that extend beyond specific applications. Understanding and addressing these implications, such as changes in economic inequality, access to AI benefits, and potential impacts on marginalized communities, are important for promoting equitable and inclusive deployment of AI systems.

Ensuring equitable distribution of AI benefits: It is crucial to ensure that the benefits of AI technologies are distributed equitably across society. Addressing issues related to accessibility, fairness, and biases in AI deployment can help prevent the exacerbation of existing inequalities and promote broad societal benefits.

Section 10.5: The Journey Ahead

The future of machine learning holds immense potential and exciting possibilities. Here are reflections on the journey ahead and key areas for further exploration:

Continued advancements in deep learning: Deep learning

architectures and techniques will continue to evolve, enabling even more complex and powerful models. Advancements in areas such as attention mechanisms, memory-augmented networks, and unsupervised learning will contribute to the development of more robust and capable AI systems.

Integration with other disciplines: Integration of machine learning with other disciplines, such as neuroscience and cognitive science, will deepen our understanding of human intelligence and potentially lead to the development of AI systems with human-like understanding, reasoning, and decision-making capabilities.

Development of AI systems with human-like understanding: While achieving human-level AI remains a grand challenge, progress will be made in developing AI systems that exhibit advanced capabilities in understanding natural language, perceiving the environment, and reasoning. Such advancements will drive the development of more sophisticated AI applications.

Continued focus on ethical considerations: The ethical implications of AI will remain at the forefront of research and development efforts. Striving for ethical and responsible AI development practices, addressing biases and fairness concerns, ensuring transparency and accountability, and promoting public engagement in AI decision-making will be critical.

Collaboration between academia, industry, and policymakers: Collaborative efforts between academia, industry, and policymakers are vital to address challenges, shape AI regulations, and foster responsible AI development. Effective partnerships and interdisciplinary research will drive innovation and ensure that AI technologies are developed and deployed in a manner that benefits society as a whole.

Impact on various sectors: Machine learning will continue to impact various sectors, including healthcare, transportation, finance, and education. Advancements in AI will transform these sectors, leading to improvements in diagnosis and treatment, autonomous vehicles, personalized finance services, and adaptive education systems.

As the field of machine learning continues to progress, embracing the challenges and opportunities that lie ahead, addressing ethical considerations, and fostering collaboration and interdisciplinary research will shape the future of AI and unlock its full potential for the benefit of humanity.